SECRET JOURNEY

POEMS AND PRAYERS FROM
ROUND THE WORLD

COMPILED AND ILLUSTRATED BY

SUSAN SKINNER

Copyright © 2005 O Books
O Books is an imprint of The Bothy, John Hunt Publishing Ltd.,
Deershot Lodge, Park Lane, Ropley, Hants, SO24 0BE, UK
office@johnhunt-publishing.com
www.O-books.net

Distribution in:
UK
Orca Book Services
orders@orcabookservices.co.uk
Tel: 01202 665432 Fax: 01202 666219 Int. code (44)

USA and Canada
NBN
custserv@nbnbooks.com
Tel: 1 800 462 6420 Fax: 1 800 338 4550

Australia
Brumby Books
sales@brumbybooks.com
Tel: 61 3 9761 5535 Fax: 61 3 9761 7095

New Zealand
Peaceful Living
books@peaceful-living.co.nz
Tel: 64 7 57 18105 Fax: 64 7 57 18513

Singapore
STP
davidbuckland@tlp.com.sg
Tel: 65 6276 Fax: 65 6276 7119

South Africa
Alternative Books
altbook@global.co.za
Tel: 27 011 792 7730 Fax: 27 011 972 7787

Text and illustrations: © Susan Skinner
Bieldside, West Furlong Lane, Hurstpierpoint, W Sussex BN6 9RH

Design: BookDesign™, London

ISBN 1 905047 08 8

A CIP catalogue record for this book is available from the British Library.

Printed in Singapore by Tien Wah Press (PTE) Limited

SECRET JOURNEY

POEMS AND PRAYERS FROM ROUND THE WORLD

COMPILED AND ILLUSTRATED BY

SUSAN SKINNER

BOOKS

WINCHESTER UK
NEW YORK USA

To Paul Who Keeps the Faith

Acknowledgements

I would like to thank Thames and Hudson Ltd. for permission to quote from The Mystic Spiral by Jill Purce 1992 C) Jill Purce 1974; Brid Fitzpatrick, co-author with Wa-Na-Nee-Che, for quotations from Great Grandfather Spirit published by HarperCollins; the University of Oklahoma Press for a quotation from Black Elk by Steltenkamp reprinted by permission of the publisher; and all those whom I have been unsuccessful in contacting.

Contents

Foreword

These prayers, verses and invocations are drawn from many faiths and many nations but they all reflect the same mystery: the mystery of our passage from birth, through life, to death. We are born from the unknown. Our life, except perhaps to our friends and family, is a secret journey of joy and sorrow. Our death is shrouded in questions.

In the words of St. Paul, '..now we see through a glass darkly..' But we do see some things, if we respond to the spirit within. Most faiths, personal or communal, acknowledge the inspiration of the spiritual life founded on truth, love and compassion.

This anthology is a small reflection of all the inspired and enlightening words that have been passed on down the centuries, throughout the world. For the folly of mankind has always been dogged by wisdom. It sing to us in every age, from east and west and north and south, like a shining bird flying at a great height who sees everything and everyone.
That song reaches out to the child within us all, to the spirit which always remains open and free and clear-sighted. In the words of Master Eckhart: 'The eye with which I see God is the same eye with which God sees me.'

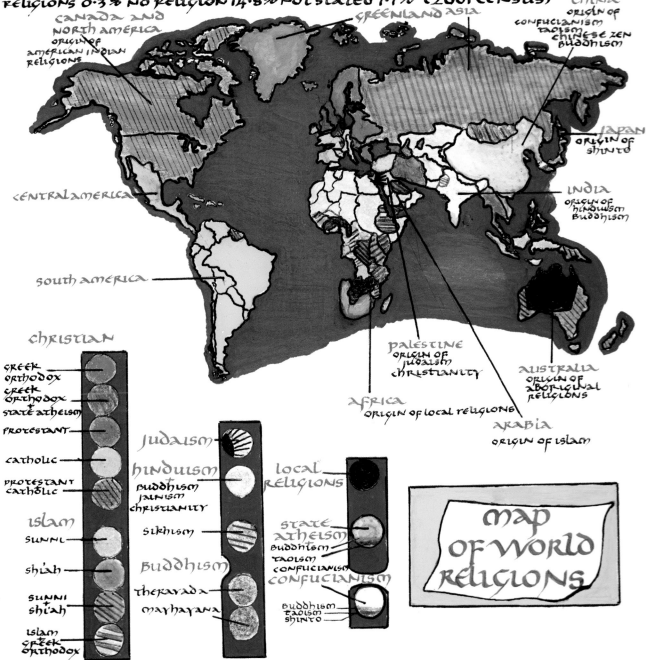

THIS MAP IS A ROUGH GUIDE: PEOPLE MOVE ABOUT THE WORLD AND TAKE THEIR RELIGION WITH THEM. PEOPLE ALSO RESPOND TO POLITICAL CHANGE. ONLY A CENSUS GIVES DETAIL. FOR EXAMPLE A CENSUS IN ENGLAND AND WALES REVEALED: CHRISTIAN 71·7% BUDDHIST 0·3% HINDU 1·1% JEWISH 0·5% MUSLIM 3·0% SIKH 0·6% OTHER RELIGIONS 0·3% NO RELIGION 14·8% NOT STATED 7·7% (2001 CENSUS)

CANADA AND NORTH AMERICA
ORIGIN OF AMERICAN INDIAN RELIGIONS

GREENLAND

ASIA

CHINA
ORIGIN OF CONFUCIANISM TAOISM CHINESE ZEN BUDDHISM

JAPAN
ORIGIN OF SHINTO

CENTRAL AMERICA

INDIA
ORIGIN OF HINDUISM BUDDHISM

SOUTH AMERICA

PALESTINE
ORIGIN OF JUDAISM CHRISTIANITY

AFRICA
ORIGIN OF LOCAL RELIGIONS

AUSTRALIA
ORIGIN OF ABORIGINAL RELIGIONS

ARABIA
ORIGIN OF ISLAM

CHRISTIAN

GREEK ORTHODOX
GREEK ORTHODOX + STATE ATHEISM
PROTESTANT
CATHOLIC
PROTESTANT CATHOLIC

ISLAM
SUNNI
SHI'AH
SUNNI + SHI'AH
ISLAM GREEK ORTHODOX

JUDAISM

HINDUISM
BUDDHISM JAINISM CHRISTIANITY

SIKHISM

BUDDHISM
THERAVADA
MAHAYANA

LOCAL RELIGIONS

STATE ATHEISM
BUDDHISM
TAOISM
CONFUCIANISM

CONFUCIANISM

BUDDHISM
TAOISM
SHINTO

MAP OF WORLD RELIGIONS

Reflections on A Journey

Give me my scallop shell of quiet
My staff of faith to walk upon,
My scrip of joy, immortal diet,
My bottle of salvation,
My gown of glory, hope's true gage;
And thus I'll take my pilgrimage.

An Inch Square

Between the sun and moon there is a field an inch square which is the heavenly heart, the dwelling of light, the golden flower.

Birth

Our birth is but a sleep and a forgetting:
The Soul that rises with us, our life's Star,
Hath had elsewhere it's setting,
And cometh from afar:
Not in entire forgetfulness,
And not in utter nakedness,
but trailing clouds of glory do we come,
From God, who is our home:
Heaven lies about us in our infancy!

Song of The Women of Mali

AIR BLOWS ONTO WATER— WATER DROPS FORM BEINGS
MUDOGON GUIDE SIGN

To have a child, to have a child, O men.
To have a child, to have a child.
What I want is a child.
Yes, even if you have put gold
in the ears of your wife,
it is the child who adorns a woman.

Speak to Us of Children

And a woman who held a babe against her bosom said,
Speak to us of children.
And he said:
Your children are not your children.
They are the sons and daughters of Life's longing for itself.
They come through you but not from you,
And though they are with you yet they belong not to you.
You may give them your love but not your thoughts,
For they have their own thoughts.
You may house their bodies but not their souls,
For their souls dwell in the house of tomorrow
which you cannot visit, not even in your dreams.

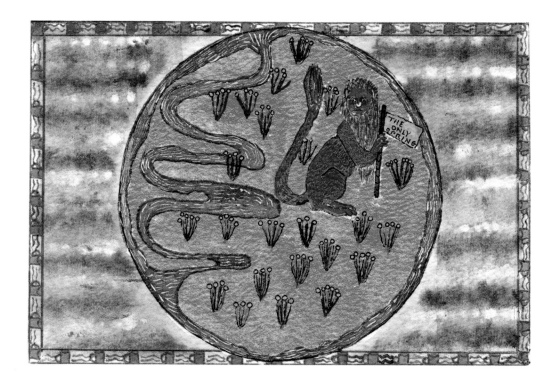

Christ the Lion

'Are you not thirsty?' said the Lion.
'I'm dying of thirst,' said Jill.
'Then drink,' said the Lion.
'May I - could I - would you mind going away while I do?' said Jill.
The Lion answered this only by a look and a very low growl…
'I daren't come and drink,' said Jill.
'Then you will die of thirst,' said the Lion.
'Oh dear!' said Jill, coming another step nearer. 'I suppose I must go and look for
another stream then.'
'There is no other stream,' said the Lion.

Little Lamb

Little Lamb, who made thee?
Dost thou know who made thee?
Gave thee life and bid thee feed
By the stream and o'er the mead;
Gave thee clothing of delight,
Softest clothing, woolly, bright:
Gave thee such a tender voice,
Making all the vales rejoice?
Little Lamb, who made thee?
Dost thou know who made thee?

Birth

I was born upon the prairie
Where the wind blew free
And there was nothing
To break the light of the sun.
I was born where everything
Drew a free breath.

PIPE OF PEACE

Thy Child

Even if I have gone astray, I am thy child, O God;
Thou art my father and mother.

Father and Mother

Who is my mother, who is my father?
Only Thou, O God.

The Virgin

Over the hilltop
And over the town
The Virgin goes walking
With Stars in her gown.
Stars on her left hand
And stars on her right,
She wakes with the twilight
And walks in the night

To the Sun

All cattle rest in their pastures,
The trees and the plants flourish,
The birds flutter in their marshes,
Their wings uplifted in adoration to thee.
All the sheep dance upon their feet,
All winged things fly,
They live when thou hast shone upon them.

A Child's Prayer

O Lord Jesus Christ, who received the children who came to Thee,
Receive also from me, Thy child, this evening prayer.
Shelter me under the shadow of Thy wings,
That in peace I may lie down and sleep.
And wake me in due time, so that I may glorify Thee,
For Thou alone art righteous and merciful.

Love

When I was a child, I spake as a child, I understood as a child, I thought as a
child: but when I became a man, I put away childish things.
For now we see through a glass darkly; but then face to face to face: now I know
in part; but then shall I know even as also I am known.
And now abideth faith, hope, love, these three; but the greatest of these is love.

One Step at A Time

The journey of a thousand miles starts from beneath your feet.

Golden String

I will give you the end of the golden string,
Only wind it into a ball,
It will lead you in at Heaven's Gate
Built in Jerusalem's wall.

The Dance

Dance, dance wherever you may be,
I am the Lord of the Dance said he,
And I'll lead you all wherever you may be
I'll lead you all in the Dance, said he.

THE SUN FLOWER
THE INDIAN SUN
THE GOLDEN
FLOWER OF PERU

 Purpose

Everything on the earth has a purpose,
Every disease a herb to cure it,
And every person a mission.
This is the Indian theory of existence.

The Pearl

The pearl sought by the pilgrim Sudama is the Golden City of
Krishna. His quest for enlightenment is a long and difficult journey that
is echoed and affirmed by man.

The Bright Field

I have seen the sun break through
to illuminate a small field
for a while, and gone my way
and forgotten it. But that was the pearl
of great price, the one field that had
the treasure in it.

Wings

You are to me O Lord
What wings are to the flying bird.

The Fly

Seeest thou the little winged fly, smaller than a grain of sand?
It has a heart like thee, a brain open to heaven and hell.
Within, wondrous and expansive;
its gates are not closed:
I hope thine are not.

Ancient Teachings

They will return,
They will return again
All over the Earth.
They are returning again.
Ancient teachings of the Earth.
They are returning again.
I give them to you
And through them
You will understand,
You will see.
They are returning again
Upon the Earth.

Within the illustration:

JESUS saith unto him, whom the Father will send in my name, He shall the WAY the TRUTH and, the LIFE if a man love me He will keep my words and my father will love him all things to your remembrance whatsoever I have said to you. PEACE I leave with you, my peace I give unto you. JOHN XIV whom the Father will love him and we will come unto him. The Comforter which is the SPIRIT

LET NOT
YOUR HEART
BE TROUBLED

The Word

Spirit of the Word, with you we enter
into the narrow way.
Spirit of the Word, with you we walk
Along the great road.

Eyes

The eye with which I see God is the same eye
with which God sees me.

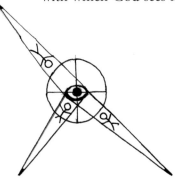

The Circle

We know that its centre is Your dwelling place.
Upon this circle the generations will walk.

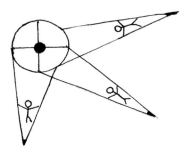

The Seeker

You are a seeker.
Delight in the mastery
Of your hands and your feet,
Of your words and your thoughts.
By day the sun shines
and the warrior in his armour shines.
By night the moon shines,
And the master shines in meditation.
By day and night
The man who is awake
Shines in the radiance of the spirit.

The Spirit

We have received, not the spirit of the world,
but the spirit which is of God;
that we might know the things
that are freely given to us of God.

The Warrior

To seek the perfection of the warrior's spirit is the only task worthy of
your manhood. The mood of a warrior calls for control over himself
and at the same time it calls for abandoning himself.

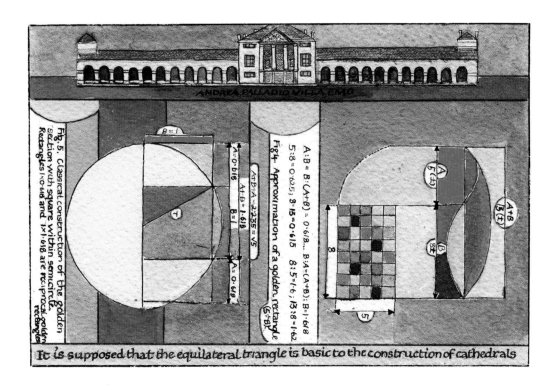

ANDREA PALLADIO VILLA EMO

Fig. 5. Classical construction of the golden section within semicircle & square. Rectangles 1×0·618 and 1×1·618 are reciprocal golden rectangles.

Fig. 4. Approximation of a golden rectangle (5:8).

B = 1
A = 0·618
A+B = 1·618
B = 1
A+B+A = 2·236 = √5
A = 0·618

A:B = B:(A+B) = 0·618... B:A=(A+B):B)=1·618
5:8 = 0·625; 8:13 = 0·615   8:5 = 1·6; 13:8 = 1·62

A (5+3)
A+B (13÷8)
B (8÷5)
8
5

It is supposed that the equilateral triangle is basic to the construction of cathedrals

The Student

Every diagram, system of numbers, every scheme of harmony,
every law of the movement of the stars
ought to appear as one to those who study in the right way.

Committed Love

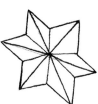

Let me not to the marriage of true minds
Admit impediments. Love is not love
Which alters when it alteration finds,
Or bends with the remover to remove.
O no! it is an ever-fixed mark,
That looks on tempests and is never shaken;
It is the star to every wandering bark,
Whose worth's unknown although his height be taken.
Love's not time's fool, though rosy lips and cheeks
Within his bending sickle's compass come;
Love alters not with his brief hours and weeks,
But bears it out even to the edge of doom.
If this be error, and upon me proved
I never writ, nor no man ever loved.

A Thing of Beauty

A thing of beauty is a joy forever:
Its loveliness increases; it will never
Pass into nothingness; but still will keep
A bower quiet for us, and a sleep
Full of sweet dreams, and health, and quiet breathing.

Summer

Summer and its days long and slow,
A herd of thick-maned horses.
The beauty of the word which the Trinity speaks,
Beautiful too when old age comes.

Life

What is life?
It is the flash of a firefly in the night.
It is the breath of a buffalo in the winter time.
It is the shadow which runs across the grass
And loses itself in the Sunset.

Pilgrims

We are strangers before thee, and sojourners,
as were all our fathers: our days on the earth are
as a shadow, and there is none abiding.

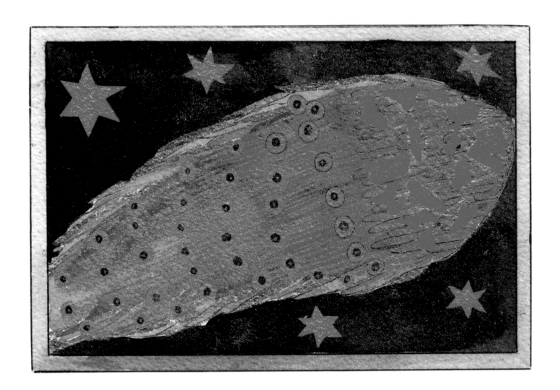

The Evening Sun

Creator, the evening sun sets on each one of us.
Our days draw to a sleepy close.
All the colours of the night sky beckon
And we follow on its brilliant yellow-red wing.
Creator, all those we have ever loved surround us,
We offer thanks and prayers for each one.

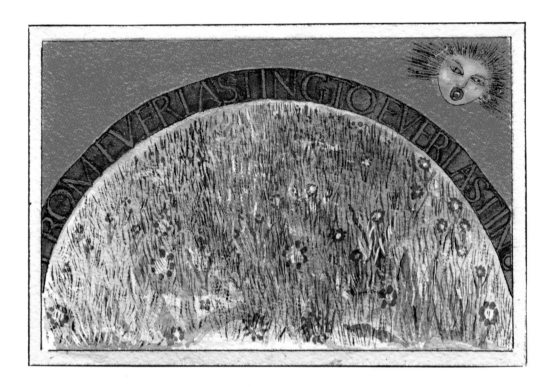

God's Mercy

As for man, his days are as grass;
as a flower of the field,
so he flourisheth.
For the wind passeth over it, and it is gone,
and the place thereof shall know it no more.
But the mercy of the Lord is from
everlasting to everlasting.

God's Comfort

The Lord is my shepherd; I shall not want. He maketh me to lie
down in green pastures: he leadeth me beside the still waters. He
restoreth my soul: he leadeth me in the paths of righteousness for his
name's sake. Yea, though I walk through the valley of the shadow of
death, I will fear no evil: for thou art with me; thy rod and thy staff
they comfort me.

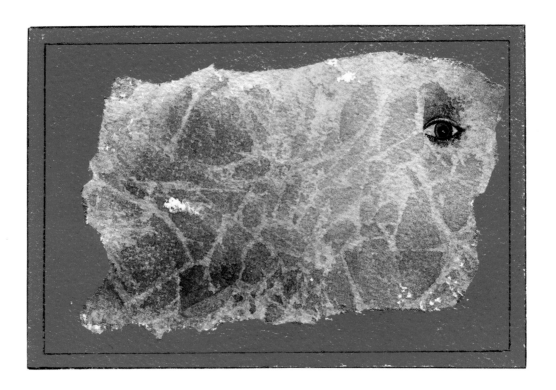

Ever Present

O Thou who art veiled in the shrouds of Thy Glory,
so that no eye can perceive Thee!
O Thou who shineth forth in the perfection of Thy splendour,
So that our hearts realise Thy Majesty!
How shall Thou be hidden, seeing that Thou art ever Manifest:
Or how shalt Thou be absent, seeing that Thou art ever Present
And watchest over us?

Enter Paradise with delight

Paradise

Enter paradise, you and your spouses, in all delight. To them will be
passed golden dishes and golden cups. There will be all that souls
desire and all that eyes delight in. There you shall abide forever. Such
is the Paradise you shall inherit, by virtue of your good deeds. You
shall have therein abundant fruit.

God's Spirit

With wide-embracing love
Thy spirit animates eternal years,
Pervades and broods above,
Changes, sustains, dissolves, creates and rears.

Though earth and moon were gone
And suns and universes ceased to be
And Thou wert left alone
Every Existence would exist in Thee.

Be Still

Be still and know that I am God

NOTES

1   Reflections on a journey: Walter Raleigh : 1552-1618

He was a courtier, adventurer, poet and historian. Born in Devon he studied at Oriel College Oxford. He fought in France and Ireland and became a favourite of Queen Elizabeth 1st. He organized several voyages of exploration and colonization to the Americas. He unsuccessfully tried to colonize Virginia but at least brought about the introduction of tobacco and potatoes to England. When his secret marriage to Elizabeth Throckmorton, one of the queen's ladies-in-waiting, became public with the birth of their son in 1592, he was imprisoned for a brief time in the Tower of London. In 1595 he explored the coastline of Trinidad, sailed the Orinoco and took part in the sack of Cadiz. In 1603 he was arrested on suspicion of conspiracy to murder James 1st.He was condemned to death but at the last minute committed to the tower where he lived with his wife until 1616. He was released to make an expedition to the Orinoco in search of gold. He failed, lost his son and his fleet, and in 1618 his suspended death sentence was evoked and he was beheaded. This quotation is the first verse of 'The Passionate Man's Pilgrimage' with its subtitle, 'supposed to be written by one at the point of death.' The shell is a sign for a prosperous journey. In Medieval allegories the shell is always associated with pilgrims and pilgrimages.

2   Inch square: from 'The Secret of the Golden Flower,' Liao Dynasty, China 907-1125

In the square thoughts are gathered and light circulated into a spiritual body. This Light-body is the flaming pearl, the symbol of spiritual knowledge and enlightenment. The sun and the moon represent two eyes.

3   Birth : Intimations of Mortality from Recollections of Early Childhood : William Wordsworth: 1770-1850

As a child William Wordsworth was sent to Hawksworth in the Lake District in the North of England to be educated. He never forgot the freedom and happiness he felt there. He grew up to be one of England's great innovative poets, opposing the previous classical tradition and exploring the lives of humble people who were in contact with nature, unaffected by the rebellious times in which they lived. Wordsworth himself was a political radical until his revolutionary sympathies were discouraged by Napoleon's ambitions.

Lyrical Ballads (1798) was a collection of poems by Wordsworth and Coleridge that reflected their new 'romantic' attitude. It begins with Coleridge's 'Ancient Mariner' and ends with Wordsworth's Tintern Abbey. Wordsworth wrote many fine poems including 'The Prelude' (1805) that remained unpublished until after his death. His sister Dorothy was always a great help to him. He married Mary Hutchinson in 1802 and became poet Laureate in 1843. The painting shows the celestial light that streams down on every new-born baby.

4   Song of the Women of Mali : African Chant

Mali is a landlocked country in North West Africa. It is very poor although the Inland Niger Delta encourages rice growing and there is enough pasture elsewhere for cattle, sheep and goats. This song expresses the people's love and need for children above any wealth. In the painting the mother has only eyes for her child – the most precious jewel of all.

5   Speak to us of children from The Prophet: Khalil Gibran 1883-1931

He was born in Lebanon but emigrated to Boston in the United States in 1895. In 1898 he returned to his native Beirut so that he could carry on his studies. He returned to Boston in 1903 where he published his first literary essays. From then on he devoted himself to painting and writing. He wrote in both Arabic and English in a romantic and mystical style that proved very popular. The painting depicts children leaving their mother, as they must, and going, in Gibran's words, into 'The house of tomorrow.'

6   Christ the Lion: C.S.Lewis 1898-1963

He published many books on theology and literary concerns, also the story of his short-lived marriage that was made into a play called Shadowlands. In 1950 he began to write fantasy stories about the land of Narnia, a magical place that was reached through an old wardrobe. The children meet all sorts of characters there, including Aslan, the great Lion Saviour. He wrote seven volumes that have become an ever favourite childrens' classic. This quotation is from 'The Silver Chair', the second to last book in the series. In the painting Aslan is standing by the River of Life that encircles the world.

7   Little Lamb: William Blake 1757-1827

British poet, painter, engraver and mystic. He was born in London, the son of an Irish hosier. He was apprenticed to the engraver James Basire, then studied at the Royal Academy School. He earned his living as a journeyman engraver and illustrator, specializing in water colour illustrations. He became a prolific poet. His first book of poems was Poetical Sketches (1783) followed by Songs of Innocence (1789) and Songs of Experience (1794) in which he wrote beautiful lyrics that expressed his belief in freedom and his dislike of materialism. He engraved twenty-seven plates for Songs of Innocence, transferring text and illustration on to etched copper plates with the desire to present his art and poetry as a whole. This excerpt from The Lamb is found in the Songs of Innocence. In the poem the lamb and the child are both symbols of innocence and of religion. However, it is the child who asks the questions and answers them. In the painting the lamb is looking up at the child who is standing with us, outside the picture, since we too ask the same sort of questions.

8   Birth: Ten Bears of the Comanche Tribe

The Comanche are a North American Uto-Aztecan Indian people. They lived in the plains and prairies of Oklahoma and Texas. They were an offshoot of the Shoshone Tribe and migrated from the Rocky mountains in Canada to hunt buffalo. Their name means 'wide trail.' In the painting the tipi is decorated with an eagle motif for the eagle embodies the power of Wakan Tanka, the Great Spirit. For Native Americans a name holds reality inside itself.

9   Thy Child: Sikh Arjan d. 606

The Sikhs, from the Punjab, (a fertile plain in N.W India and Pakistan, traversed by the Indus and five tributaries) were a sect who dissented from Brahmanical Hinduism, a complex and sacrificial religion that emerged around 900BC. Their Founder was Guru Nanak (1469).He believed in One God and taught that the outward show of religion was worthless. Sikhism combines elements of

Hinduism and Islam, taking on the Hindu concept of reincarnation and karma (the moral law of cause and effect by which a person's status in life is determined by his deeds in a previous life) but rejecting the caste system (in which people are grouped according to social rank.)

9   Father and Mother:

A quotation from the American-Indian Kekchi Tribe. The painting shows a child looking up at God, who is Father and Mother.

10   The Virgin: Eleanor Farjeon 1881-1965

She was a childrens' story writer and poet who won the Carnegie and the Hans Christian Anderson Medal for services to childrens' literature. This poem is one of her Zodiac Songs. Virgo is the sixth sign of the zodiac (August 23rd - September 22nd.) The painting shows the Virgin as Mary flying across the sky.

11   To the Sun: An Egyptian hymn

This is from a hymn to Aten, the supreme god and creative principle of ancient Egypt. Aten (the sun god) was worshipped during the reign of King Amenhotep, who changed his name to Akhenaten (c1353-1335 BC) He is symbolised by the sun's disk. He built a new city for himself and for his god at Amarna, and called it Akhetaten. Although it became a centre of artistic activity Akhenaten's empire weakened and after his death Aten worship ceased.

12   A child's prayer: from the Greek Orthodox Church

The Greek Orthodox Church separated from the Roman Catholic Church in the 11th century. Differences of opinion in how the Creed was recited led to 'the East-West schism'. In the West it was said the Holy Spirit proceeded from the Father and the Son. In the East it was said the Holy Spirit proceeded from the Father only. In the 11th century theological differences between the East and West Churches were possibly cultural and linguistic, rather than based on a different view of the Divinity.

13   Love: St. Paul (1st century) from St Paul's letter to the Corinthians1 chapter13 verses 11-13

Paul was the Apostle to the Gentiles (non-Jewish people). At fourteen he trained as a rabbi and also learned to be a tent-maker. He persecuted Christians, including St. Stephen, but on his way to Damascus he had a vision of Jesus Christ and converted to the Christian faith. He made three missions to the Gentiles and wrote letters to the people of the new churches, such as the Galatians, the Romans and the Corinthians. (Corinth is in the northeast Peloponnesus on the gulf of Corinth, Greece.) Paul had many adventures and after a fanatical outcry against him from the Jews he was brought to Caesaria and tried by the procurator Felix. He was imprisoned for two years but as a Roman citizen he appealed to Caesar. In 62 AD he was put under house arrest in Rome and executed under the Roman Emperor Nero.

14   One step at a time: Lao-tzu (sixth century BC) from the Tao Te Ching (the Way of Power)

Taoism is one of the three main Chinese religions, along with Buddhism and and Confucianism. It emphasises the need for inner contemplation, mystical forms of knowledge and non-active, spontaneous union with the nature of being, the ultimate reality. It has its own religious, philosophical and ritualistic traditions. Through silence, stillness and actionless action, known as wu wei the Taoist aims to achieve unity with the Tao.

15   Golden String: William Blake 1757-1827
This quotation is the first verse of 'Epigraph'. (See notes on Blake: Little Lamb)

16   The Dance: from a Shaker hymn
The Shakers (so called because of their shaking movements during religious ecstasy), are allied to the Quakers, a Christian movement that rejects the formal structures of creed and sacraments and relies on each individual's inner light. In 1758 Anne Lee was inspired, through her visions, to call herself the female Christ. She set up a community near Albany, in New York. The Shakers have a reputation for being excellent crafts people.

17   Purpose: Mourning Dove (1888-1936) Salish Tribe
Native American people have always considered the purpose of plants and herbs is both for healing and consumption. The Sunflower, or Indian Sun, depicted in the painting, first grew in Peru and different parts of America from where it was brought into Europe. The buds were sometimes floured and boiled. Among the many plants used for healing (by experienced medical people) were alfalfa or buffalo herb, to renew energy, and aspen, whose inner bark was ground down into a fine powder, mixed with hot water and made into a tea for fevers, bad colds and persistent coughs. Bloodroot, lavender, cedar, coltsfoot, daisy, dandelion, honeysuckle and many other plants have been used by Native Americans to eat, drink or heal.

18   The Pearl: Description of a painting Punjab Hills India c1785
The function of the pearl is to represent the mystic centre and sublimation. In this case the mystic centre is Krishna and the pilgrim is on his way to find him. In the Hindu religion Krishna (Sanscrit for black) is the eighth incarnation or avatar of the Hindu god Vishnu who preserves the cosmos and restores moral order. The worship of Vishnu is widely embraced in modern Hinduism. In the painting the pilgrim is rowing down the sacred river Ganges, keeping his vision in mind.

19   From The Bright Field: R.S.Thomas 1913-2000
Ronald Stuart Thomas was born in Cardiff and educated at the University College of North Wales, Bangor, where he studied Classics. He then went to St. Michael's College, Llandaff to train for the Church. In 1937 he was ordained as a clergyman in the Church of Wales and worked in rural parishes. He has published many collections of poetry but only became known outside Wales with the publication of Song at the Year's Turning (1955). He is a leading Anglo-Welsh poet who sees life, for all its difficulties, as 'stubborn with beauty.'

20   Wings: from a disciple of Ramakrishna (1836-1886)
Ramakrishna was an Indian yogi and mystic. In his teachings he condemned lust, money and the caste system (in which people are grouped according to specific social rank). He preached that all religions leading to the attainment of mystical experience are equally good and true. His ideas were spread through Europe and the USA by his disciple Vivekananda. In this quotation the author is

expressing the freedom he feels in his belief.

21   The Fly: William Blake 1757-1827 from Milton, book1 line24

William Blake was a visionary who often drew his inspiration from the natural world. The painting of the fly might encourage us, to see, as Blake does, how delicate and beautiful this much despised creature is. (see notes for Little Lamb)

22   Ancient Teachings:Crazy Horse Sioux Chief 1849-1877

The Oglala Sioux of the North American Plains studied and revered animals and used the lessons they learned to become skilful hunters. The Oglala culture is about relationship with family, clan, tribal group, land, animals, plants, and all the elements, sky, wind, clouds that make up the whole universe. This is what is meant by the old teaching that Crazy Horse says will return. Crazy Horse himself was a great warrior. In 1876 he led a successful rearguard action of Sioux and Cheyenne warriors, invading the US army forces in Montana. Shortly afterwards Crazy Horse and his men joined Sitting Bull at Little Big Horn where he played an important part in the massacre of General Custer's US forces. However he had to surrender in 1877 and was killed a few months later while he was in custody in Nebraska.

23   The Word: Part of a Ritual from Gabon (an equatorial country on Africa's Atlantic coast)

This ritual is spoken by those who aspire to become judge, ambassador or orator to the people of Gabon. They have to belong to an association called Evovi (translation) To do this they must go through a rite called 'The Gift of the Word.' They are gathered together in a courtyard for about a week round a reliquary containing the skull of an ancestral member of the order. During the retreat they dance and sing and listen to the secret wise words of older members. On the eighth day all the Evovi leave the courtyard tapping the ground with the points of their ebony sticks and singing about the Spirit of the Word. The painting represents the enclosed space where the beginners circle round and go through the ceremony. It also reminds us of the closeness of the African text to the words of Jesus: Enter ye in at the strait gate: for wide is the gate, and broad is the way, that leadeth to destruction, and many there be that go in thereat; Because strait is the gate, and narrow is the way, which leadeth unto life, and few there be that find it. Matthew 7 verses 13-14

24   Eyes: A quotation from Meister Ekhart 1260-1327

He was a German mystic , born in Hochheim. He became a Dominican monk and studied and taught in Paris. In 1307 he became Vicar-General of Bohemia. He taught a form of mystical pantheism in which God and Nature are identified as one. In 1325 the Archbishop of Cologne accused him of heresy and after his death his writings were condemned by Pope John XX11. He had a big influence on later religious mysticism and philosophy.

25   The Circle: Black Elk 1863-1950

He was an Oglala Sioux, a distant cousin of Crazy Horse and a mystic, who from the age of nine, had repeated visions. He became a medicine man and a healer. The Nebraskan poet and intellectual, John G Neihardt, visited Black Elk in 1930 and wrote down his oral biography. (Black Elk Speaks.) Black Elk was said to be the last Sioux to have a complete knowledge and understanding of the Sioux religion. The essentials of its most important rituals were published in 1953 (The Sacred Pipe: Joseph E. Brown.) The painting depicts curtains drawn to reveal a circle in which all geometric forms are related and on which little figures are standing. It is vaguely reminiscent of a Celtic Christian decoration, reminding us that in some way or another most religions are connected.

26 The Seeker: from Sayings of the Buddha: Buddha c563-c483 BC

'Buddha means 'The Enlightened One.' It is the title of Prince Gautama Siddhartha, the founder of Buddhism. He was the son of the rajah (a king or prince) of the Sakya tribe who lived north of Benares, in Nepal. When Prince Gautama was about thirty years old he left the Court, his beautiful wife and all earthly ambitions, to lead the an austere life. He sat in contemplation under a banyan tree not far from Buddh Gaya Bihar, a region in north-east India. Through his long contemplation he found enlightenment. After this he gathered together disciples and taught for 40 years. Existence, he maintained, is filled with sorrow and Nirvana, or non-existence, that is reached by the Buddhistic way of life, is the ultimate good. In the painting an enlightened person is floating lightly for joy. The background represents the radiance of the spirit.

27 The Spirit: St Paul 1st century

St Paul was the apostle of the Gentiles, or non-Jewish people. At fourteen he went from Tarsus, where he was born, to Jerusalem to train as a rabbi under rabbi Gamaliel, a prominent Pharisee, who strictly observed the written law. He also learned to be a tent-maker. He persecuted Christians, including St Stephen. He was on his way to Damascus when a vision of Jesus Christ converted him to Christianity. He travelled far on his missionary work and wrote letters to the new churches he established. He confronted many difficulties that are related in the Acts of the Apostles. He was tried before the Roman procurator Felix and after two years' imprisonment he used his right as a Roman citizen to appeal to Caesar. In 62 he arrived in Rome and was under house arrest for two years after which he was executed under Nero. The painting shows an angel whispering in a man's ear about all the gifts he has been given. (see also 13 Love)

28 The Warrior: Don Juan, a contemporary Mexican shaman

The warrior is a symbol for all of us, both in life and what we do in life. The balance between control and abandonment gives us mastery and trust in our destiny, and a means of perfecting whatever work we wish to achieve. We must learn the rules but be prepared to act spontaneously, with confidence and without thought. This is, for example, how we learn to ride a bicycle. The painting on the left represents a medieval warrior as he rides his horse to battle. His posture shows us he is both in control and yet acting with freedom. The painting on the right shows us the warrior in a temple. He is in meditation, where his thoughts run freely but are constantly returning to the worship of God.

29 The Student: Plato c. 428-c. 348 BC

Plato is one of the most influential philosophers of all time. Socrates was his teacher and Aristotle was his student. These three were the philosophical geniuses of the ancient Greek world. Plato was probably born in Athens into an aristocratic family. When Socrates was condemned to death in 399 BC Plato wrote of his trial and last days in three dialogues: The Apology, the Crito and the Phaedo. For a while he took refuge with Euclides, another philosopher, then he travelled widely and returned to Athens c. 387 BC to found the Academy, a place for scientific, philosophical and mathematical research. His system of thought has had a profound influence on Christian theology and Western philosophy. An example of this is his theory of 'forms' or ideas, where the transient, material world of particulars, which are merely objects of belief, opinion and perception, are contrasted with the timeless and unchanging world of universal ideas which are the objects of true knowledge. The painting depicts harmonious systems of building that reflect the universal idea of harmony.

30   Committed Love from sonnet 116 : William Shakespeare 1564-1616

He was the eldest son of John Shakespeare, glover and wool dealer. He lived in Stratford-on-Avon, Warwickshire and probably went to Stratford Grammar School. When he was eighteen he married Anne Hathaway and had three children by her: Susannah, and twins, Hamnet (who died aged 11) and Judith. He worked in London as a playwright and actor and in 1592, when the plague closed the theatres he wrote two narrative poems and 104 sonnets that were circulated in literary and courtly circles. The sonnets are among the world's finest poems. When the theatres re-opened Shakespeare joined the newly formed Lord Chamberlain's Men and had a share in company profits. Between 1594 and 1598 he wrote nine plays. He became wealthy and bought New Place, a mansion in Stratford. In London the Chamberlain's men, moved to the Globe. There Shakespeare wrote fourteen more plays and revived former works. The company, who performed to Queen Elizabeth and to James 1st, became known as the King's Men. They acted Shakespeare's plays at court and in 'private' roofed theatres. The King's Men took over one of these, the Blackfriars, and performed there in the winter. On the death of his parents Shakespeare became head of the family and by 1612 he left the management of the theatre to his 'fellows.' He had one grand-daughter from his daughter Susannah who married a well known physician, John Hall. After Shakespeare's death, two of his fellow actors, John Hemminge and Henry Condell collected and published his plays. The painting portrays the star of commitment guiding the wandering bark.

31   A Thing of Beauty from Endymion Book One: John Keats 1795-1821

He was the son of a livery stable keeper and went to school in Enfield, North London. At sixteen he was apprenticed to a surgeon in nearby Edmonton. He became a medical student for two years then turned to poetry. Leigh Hunt published his first sonnets in the Examiner and in 1818 Keats' long mythological poem Endymion was published.It was savagely reviewed. He fell in love with Fanny Brawne and in 1820 published 'Lamia and other poems.' This volume included his beautiful odes. It was to become a landmark collection in the history of English poetry. Keats wrote many letters that are very important as they throw great light on his poetic development. He looked after his younger brother Tom, who was dying of consumption. Keats died of the same illness in Rome in a house by the Spanish steps. (26 Piazza di Spagna.) In his honour the house is dedicated to English Romantic poetry.

32   Summer: An old Celtic prayer from a 13th century Welsh poem.

The Celts are West European people, who include pre-Roman inhabitants of Britain and Gaul (modern day France) and their descendants, found mainly in Ireland, Scotland, Wales, Cornwall, Brittany and the Isle of Man. The Celtic language is divided into two groups. The first is called Goidelic (Irish, Scots, Gaelic, Manx) and the second Brythonic (Welsh, Cornish, Breton) From the fifth to the seventh century the Celtic Church in Ireland was the most important Christian centre in Northern Europe. Its missionaries established monasteries in the North of England (on the islands of Iona and Lindisfarne) and as far afield as Italy and Gaul.They also re-evangelised England. Celtic prayer is imbued with an awareness of the natural world.

33 Life: Crowfoot of the Blackfoot tribe, Ojibway nation, as he prepared for his journey to the spirit world in 1890

According to Ojibway belief, the spirit begins its long and difficult walk on a well-beaten path that leads it westward to the Goodlands. On arrival, all the relatives and ancestors since the beginning of mankind are gathered in a welcoming party to greet the spirit.

34 Pilgrims: Old Testament Chronicles 1 chapter 29 verse 15

According to Jewish tradition Ezra was the author of Chronicles or they may have been written by a Levite connected with the musical services of the second temple. The object of the two books of Chronicles is to compose an individual work from a levitical and religious standpoint. Levites are the descendants of Levi who was one of the sons of Jacob.

35 The Evening Sun: a prayer by Mitakuye Oyasin, one of the elders of the Objiway nation.

He wrote about the Objiway Passing Away Ceremony and concludes: We are bound, as two leggeds, in friendship and as brothers and sisters, to sustain life on this wondrous earth with dignity and honour. It is the energy that lives on whilst the body disappears back to its roots protected by the trees and the earth. The circular energy of life closes around each one of us like a blanket, as our energy is recalled to the Source and we are all one. For we are all related.

36 God's Mercy: Psalm 103 a psalm of David verses 15-17

The psalms were compiled between the sixth and second centuries BC. David was thought to be a pioneer of psalmody and his name heads various psalms, like this one. The psalms vary. They include lamentations, songs of praise, expressions of faith, resignation and joy in God's presence. There are personal psalms and others that are reflections on God's moral government and His goodness. They were and are used in public and private devotion and present an understanding of religious life and thought in Israel. They have an important place in Christian worship and, because of the great beauty of the Authorised King James version, a high place in English religious poetry.

37 God's Comfort: psalm 23 verses 1-4

See above

38 Ever Present: Ibn 'Ata' Allah, Sufi, d 1309

The name Sufism is derived from the 'suf', a simple woollen garment worn by early ascetics. Sufism is a form of Muslim mysticism. It arose in the early Islamic period (Prophet Muhammad founded Islam in the 7th century AD) as a reaction to orthodox Islamic teaching. Sufis avoid the formal rituals and learning of the doctors of theology and sacred law, in favour of practices and teachings from sheikhs (heads of religious bodies) that will lead them to direct communion with God. The central aim of Sufism is to know God directly. It has been influenced by other faiths such as Neo-Platonism and Buddhism. The painting depicts the shrouds of glory and God's eye keeping watch on us.

39 Paradise: from the Qur'an or Koran

The Qur'an is the Holy Scripture of Islam. Muslims believe it is the will and word of God that was revealed by the Angel Gabriel to Muhammad (570-632) over a period of time - from 610AD - 630 AD. It is made up of 114 chapters written in classical Arabic. The first revelation, which is called the Night of Power, is commemorated during Ramadam when Muslims abstain from food, drink, tobacco and sexual intercourse.

40   God's Spirit: from Last Lines Emily Bronte 1818-1848 poet and novelist

Emily was sister to Charlotte and Anne, who both became novelists, and Branwell who led a troubled and wayward life. The children's mother died and they were brought up by her sister in Haworth, Yorkshire, where their father became Rector. Their childhood was spent together on the wild Yorkshire moors. Branwell's twelve toy soldiers inspired the children to construct two fantasy worlds, Angria and Gondal and write them down in minute books. Their isolated, imaginative but happy childhood did not prepare the girls for the harsh regime of their first school, Cowan Bridge, though their second school, Roe head, was more suited to them. In 1837 Emily became a governess in Halifax, and in 1842 she and Charlotte attended the Heger Pensionnat in Brussels. In 1845 Charlotte discovered Emily's poems in Gondal, amongst which was Last Lines, and the sisters jointly published a book of poems under their pseudonyms Currer and Ellis Bell. Emily's novel, Wuthering Heights, was published in 1847. It is one of the best known books in the English language. The painting represents God's spirit leaning against the world and sustaining us, even at the moment of annihilation.

41   Be Still: from Psalm 46 To the Chief Musician for the Sons of Korah

Psalms 42-49 were dedicated to the sons of Korah. In Numbers, Chapter 16 we learn how Korah, one of the sons of Reuban, rose up against Moses. As a punishment, he and all the men around him, were sent down alive into a pit. The earth closed round them and suffocated them. However the sons of Korah did not die. The painting is in the form of a mandala on which to meditate.

NOTES ON MAJOR RELIGIONS

Christianity is the religion of those who follow Jesus Christ and believe him to be the Son of God. Jesus was born in Bethlehem, Palestine, and spread his gospel of faith love and hope through parables, proverbs and sermons (especially the Sermon on the Mount). From his followers in Galilee he chose twelve disciples to be his companions and to teach his message. He was betrayed by one of them (Judas Iscariot), condemned to death by the Sanhedrin, the highest Jewish court, and the Roman Governor, Pontius Pilate. He was crucified and buried but after three days his followers found his tomb empty and saw him again as a living person. Belief in his resurrection spread and his disciples now recognised Jesus as the Messiah or Christ. Christian communities grew up around Jerusalem and St Paul converted many gentiles (non Jews.) By the third century AD Christianity was widespread throughout the Roman Empire: in 313A.D. Emperor Constantine ended persecution and in 380A.D. Emperor Theodosius recognised Christianity as the state religion. There were disputes (often cultural and linguistic) among Christians over the status of Christ and the nature of the Trinity, (God the Father, God the Son and God the Holy Ghost) culminating in the Schism of 1054 A.D. The split was between the Western Church with the Pope as its head and the Eastern Greek Orthodox Church. From the 11th - 14th centuries, Christians went on crusades to secure Christian rule over the Muslim-controlled holy places of Palestine. In the 15th century further reforms led to the formation of breakaway Protestant Churches. The main traditions in the Christian

Church today are Greek Orthodox, Roman Catholic, Protestant and Non-conformist. In 1948 the need for unity was recognised by the setting up of the World Council of Churches.

Islam is the religion of the Muslims who believe in one God, Allah. It was founded in the 7th century A.D. in the Arabian Peninsula by the Prophet Mahomet (Muhammad) who received a series of revelations that were written down c610-32 A.D. as the Qu'ran or Koran. Muslims accept and affirm an individual surrender to God. The five pillars of Islam are: 1) Professing faith in a prescribed way. 2) Fulfilling good works in the community. 3) Praying five times a day, facing Mecca, (birthplace of Mahomet in western Saudi Arabia). 4) Giving alms to the poor and fasting during the month of Ramadam (ninth month of the Islamic calendar). 5) Going on pilgrimage to Mecca. There are two main branches of Islam called Sunni and Shiah. Sunni Muslims follow the Sunna, or rules of life according to the Sihah Satta, six authentic books of Tradition. They follow whatever Mahomet sets out as the ideal behaviour for a Muslim and believe in the first three caliphs (successors of Mahomet). Over 80 per cent of Muslims follow the Sunna. Shiites (those who follow the Shiah) reject the first three Sunni caliphs and regard Ali as Mahomet's first successor. They believe their Imams (prayer leaders in the mosque}possess Divine Light and special wisdom in matters of faith. For Shiites an Iman has the highest spiritual and temporal authority. It is bestowed on him by either Mahomet, or by one of Mahomet's direct descendants, or by Ali. Shiah Muslims are found mainly in Iraq, Iran, Lebanon and Bahrain.Sunni Muslims did not legitimise Shi'ism until 1959.
Islam is the professed religion of nearly 1,000 million people worldwide.

Judaism is the religion of the Jewish people. Jews are called to believe in and worship one God, the Creator, whose will is revealed in the Torah (the first five books of the Old Testament which contains the Ten Commandments.) This monotheism, inherited by Christianity and Islam, is at the heart of Judaism. The Jews believe that because God made a covenant with their ancestor Abraham they have a special relationship with Him. They believe that one day a Messiah will come who will gather together all the peoples of Israel and bring everlasting peace to earth. They worship in the synagogue (Greek for bringing together). Synagogues may be any shape but inside the main focus is the Ark - a cupboard in the wall facing Jerusalem, which contains the Torah. Above the Ark are two tablets with the first two words of each of the ten Commandments inscribed upon them. A lamp of perpetual light is suspended in front of the Ark, representing God's presence and the continuation of Judaism. Food and wine that is acceptable according to the Torah is called Kosher.

Hinduism is the dominant religion of India. It evolved from the teaching of the Vedas, or Hindu sacred texts. It is the world's oldest religion, dating back to at least 2000 B.C. It embraces many interpretations of God - God in nature (pantheism), the one and only God (monotheism), God as one substance with the world (monism). Dharma is the eternal law that underlies all existence. It is the moral and material order of the world and lies behind India's caste system that groups people in specific social ranks. It is however acknowledged that every individual has a soul called Atman. Karma is the law that governs the cause and effect of our actions, reaching from one life to another. Moshka is the liberation from the chain of birth, death and rebirth. There are an estimated 705 million Hindus in the world.

Buddhism was founded in north -east India in the 5th century B.C. by Siddhartha Gautama who is called the Buddha (enlightened one). Buddhism is a religion without a god. It is about the four noble truths that state: 1) All existence is suffering. 2)The cause of suffering is desire. 3) Freedom from suffering is called nirvana. 4) Nirvana is attained by following the eightfold path that combines mental discipline with moral behaviour and wisdom.

There are two main Buddhist traditions: Theravada Buddhism (teaching of the elders) that is dominant in Sri Lanka and S.E.Asia. Its canon of scripture was written in Pali, and contains the original teachings of the Buddha. Its emphasis is on individual enlightenment. The Mahayana Buddhist tradition, that spread to Central Asia, China, Japan, Java and Sumatra, stresses universal enlightment through the ideal of the bodhisattva (an enlightened being) who postpones his own salvation or nirvana for the love of others. There are about 300 million Buddhists world wide.

LESS WIDESPREAD RELIGIONS

Sikhism combines elements of Hinduism and Islam. It was founded in the 15th century by Guru Nanak (1469-1539A.D.) who was born into a Hindu family in a village near Lahore, India. As a child he learned about Islam. He underwent a religious experience that prompted him to become a wandering preacher. His aim was not to unite the Muslim and Hindu faiths but to preach spiritual liberation that could be achieved by practising an inward, disciplined meditation on the name of God. Sikhism accepts karma and reincarnation but rejects the caste system. It has one principle sacred scripture, the Adi Granth. In the Punjab (North West India and Pakistan)there are 18 million Sikhs.

Taoism is one of the three main Chinese religious and philosophical traditions. It emphasises inner contemplation, mystical forms of knowledge, and spontaneous non-active union with the nature of being. It was traditionally founded by Lao-Tzu) and developed from the 5th to the 3rd centuries B.C. Its tenets are found in the texts of the Tao Te Ching (attributed to Lao-Tzu.) The ultimate reality is the Tao, in which being and non being, life and death are aspects of the same reality. Through silence, stillness and actionless action (wu wei) the believer aims to achieve unity with the Tao. A religious Taoism grew up in the 3rd century A.D. and developed its own monastic system. Taoism borrowed the concept of reincarnation from the Buddhists, but its final goal is to become an immortal. It has become influential in Vietnam, Japan and Korea. Though it is suppressed in communist China it remains a strong influence in Chinese culture.

Confucianism is a system of ethical and philosophical teachings founded by Confucius in the 6th century BC and developed in the 4th century B.C. by Meng-tzu. Confucianism advocates love for one's fellows, filial piety, decorum, virtue and the ideal of the superior man. In 1190A.D. the four great Confucian texts were published, revitalizing Confucianism in China. A second series of texts, known as the five classics, include the I Ching. It is estimated that there are 5,800,000 followers of Confucianism in the world.

Shinto is a Japanese religion that has its roots in prehistory. It is based on the worship of ancestors and spirits of nature. In early times each tribe had its own spirit or kami. Eventually the Sun-goddess, Amaterasu, became the most important spirit. Shinto is a tolerant and adaptable religion, emphasising high standards of behaviour and daily rituals rather than any doctrine. At simple shrines worshippers rinse their hands and mouths, bow and offer food and drink. In the 19th century, in unified Japan, the emperor was thought to be a descendant of Amaterasu. He was considered divine and demanded loyalty and obedience. This form of worship encouraged extreme nationalism until, in 1945, after the second World War, under United States pressure, it was stopped by the Emperor himself. It was then replaced by the older form of Shinto. In Japan Shinto is seen as the religion of life, while Buddhism is seen as that of death. Marriages are therefore celebrated in Shinto tradition, while Buddhism is embraced for funeral rites.